THE POWER OF POETRY

Say The Word

Edited By Donna Samworth

First published in Great Britain in 2023 by:

 Young**Writers**

Young Writers
Remus House
Coltsfoot Drive
Peterborough
PE2 9BF
Telephone: 01733 890066
Website: www.youngwriters.co.uk

Printed and bound in the UK by BookPrintingUK
Website: www.bookprintinguk.com
YB0541AZ

FOREWORD

Since 1991, here at Young Writers we have celebrated the awesome power of creative writing, especially in young adults where it can serve as a vital method of expressing their emotions and views about the world around them. In every poem we see the effort and thought that each student published in this book has put into their work and by creating this anthology we hope to encourage them further with the ultimate goal of sparking a life-long love of writing.

Our latest competition for secondary school students, **The Power of Poetry,** challenged young writers to consider what was important to them and how to express that using the power of words. We wanted to give them a voice, the chance to express themselves freely and honestly, something which is so important for these young adults to feel confident and listened to. They could give an opinion, highlight an issue, consider a dilemma, impart advice or simply write about something they love. There were no restrictions on style or subject so you will find an anthology brimming with a variety of poetic styles and topics. We hope you find it as absorbing as we have.

We encourage young writers to express themselves and address subjects that matter to them, which sometimes means writing about sensitive or contentious topics. If you have been affected by any issues raised in this book, details on where to find help can be found at
www.youngwriters.co.uk/info/other/contact-lines

CONTENTS

Pranati Shastri (11)	66
Maisie Powles-Warren (11)	67
Max Bagge (11)	68
Sofia Stosic (12)	69
Keyaan Ahmed (12)	70
Zak Lawrenson (12)	71
Harriet Dingle (12)	72
Zoë Menegaz MacLean (12)	73
Charlie Ward (12)	74
Jacob Farrow (12)	75
Mia Maklakov (12)	76
Leo Beurich (13)	77
Megan Banyard (11)	78
Jake Ansbro (11)	79
Gabriela Kachoviciute (12)	80
Neve Williams (11)	81
Eva Haddon (12)	82
Willow Bradley (12)	83
Frank Olson (12)	84
Jacob Dye (11)	85
Erin Laughton (12)	86
William Hale-Sutton (12)	87
Florence Parish (11)	88
Alice Russell (12)	89
Harvey Bee (11)	90
Poppy Fitzpatrick (11)	91
Liliana Clay (11)	92
Clementine Jacobson (12)	93
Oliver Wilson (11)	94
Zach Ruiters (11)	95
Georgia Blanch (12)	96
Seth Ford (12)	97
Ruby Cammack (12)	98
Alin Finaru (12)	99
Emily Lamb (11)	100
Kitty Wilkins (13)	101
Ben Hargrave (11)	102
Aviv Chayut (12)	103
Thomas Brown (12)	104
Finley Bowyer (12)	105

Lincoln Castle Academy, Lincoln

Ksawery Zylka-Zebracki (15)	106
Evie Allen (13)	108
Braeden Uzzell (13)	109
Ashton Maksymiw-Mullen (15)	110
Lucy Jones (14)	111
Mia Sawyer (13)	112
Mason Lunn (12)	113
Holly Law (13)	114
Harvey Gleadhill (14)	115
Oliver Lacey (12)	116
Brandon Thompson (12)	117
Jack Johnson (11)	118
Romina Rizaie (12)	119
Ethan Dimelow (12)	120
Alice Bingham (12)	121
Ella Woods (13)	122
Evie Richardson (13)	123
Imogen Woodhouse (14)	124
Lukasz Mehassouel (14)	125
Amy Laughton (14)	126
Nicole Burrows (13)	127
Reegan-Jay Wells (12)	128
Bianca Preda (13)	129
Cherry A Pietrglciewicz (15)	130
Brandon Powell (13)	131

Radnor House Sevenoaks School, Sundridge

Emily Brewer (14)	132
Jessica Margrett (14)	133
James Paterson (13)	134
Oliver Mason (13)	135
Alice Watson (13)	136

St Anne's Academy, Middleton

Rio Hughes (12)	137
Faith Sanderson (13)	138
Kuba Wasilewski (13)	139
Excellent Bright (12)	140
Serena Ndlovu (12)	141

THE
POEMS

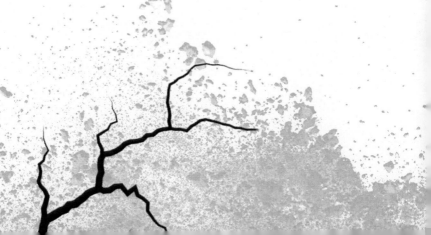

Their Legacy And Their Struggle

Have you ever killed before?
In the heat of battle,
In the heat of war,
When the bullet left the gun,
Did you feel rotten to the core?

Have you ever killed before?
The ringing in your ears,
Bringing back all your darkest fears,
Fears that linger in your mind,
Thoughts that stick for all of time.

Have you ever killed before?
The fallen that were once alive,
Trying to reason with yourself,
"I had to do that to survive!"

Have you ever killed before?
Will you win the mental war yet to come?
Your brain wants to settle the score,
The guilt is mounting,
The guilt is drowning.

We know they killed before,
For our protection,

For our freedom,
With heart, strength and conviction.

We know they killed before,
Sacrificed from Korea to 'Nam,
From Europe, to Burma, to Japan,
And in many faraway lands.

Thank you for your service,
That is what we must say,
To those whose lives have been taken away,
To the soldiers,
To the airmen,
To the sailors too.

I will remember their sacrifice
But will you?

Sam Stone (15)

Imagine A World...

Imagine a world with beautiful, growing trees,
Monkeys swinging on the branches,
Sloths hanging from the giant rainforest trees,
Howler monkeys howling as loud as they possibly can,
We can make it a reality instead of a dream,
You can make it a reality instead of a dream.

Imagine a world with beautiful, growing trees,
Orangutans eating all the mangos they can find,
Jaguars looking for tonight's dinner,
Capybaras swimming in the river,
We can make it a reality instead of a dream,
You can make it a reality instead of a dream.

Imagine a world with beautiful, growing trees,
Anteaters searching for food on the forest floor,
Amazon river dolphins cooling down in the refresh
Green iguanas camouflaging into the bright green
We can make it a reality instead of a dream,
You can make it a reality instead of a dream!

Sophie Hartley (11)
Bexhill Academy, Bexhill-On-Sea

3

World's Warning

Our world is crumbling
Climate change or global warming
It must be our world's warning

Pollution is defeating us
What can we do?
Maybe travel by train or tube
Sadly it's not that simple
And our world is warning

Icebergs are melting
Countries are scorching
Animals have lost their homes
But what do people care?
Is our world warning us about what we must repair?

Trees are going by the day
What can we say?
This madness is forever
Killing whatever
Is there a single feeling of guilt?

People are greedy
And think they need more
Our warning world is all we have

You may never leave
So treat it with kindness
For that is all we need.

Sofia Wrenn (12)
Bexhill Academy, Bexhill-On-Sea

Dear People Of The World

Dear people of the world
From left or right of the way
Come meet us now
In our small town
And help save the world today

It doesn't matter, black or white
But the world needs you now
The people in poverty or without a home
Please help to stop them from living in woe
Make an effort to save the world today

Stop thinking about the future to come
Stop thinking about the horror
And start to think about the change you could make
If the world could be saved and not be hacked

Dear people of the world, scared or brave
Please help us now and save the world today.

Ella Bassett (11)
Bexhill Academy, Bexhill-On-Sea

A Corrupt World

Corruption, deception, fraud, bribery, manipulation
It's everywhere, at every edge of the world
Earth is a dream not yet realised
Yet corruption hurts us
Deception misleads honest people
Fraud can lead to financial gain but at what cost?
You can bribe the world into thinking it's fine
You can manipulate the world into thinking it's good
But think
Does Earth want war? Do you want war?
Each battlefield is a scar on the Earth's surface
Take your blindfolds off
See our real world
Can't you see
Corruption is blinding us from the truth!

Joey Lowry (13)
Bexhill Academy, Bexhill-On-Sea

Destruction Poem

Earth is our world that we live in
We need to keep it clean
So it can stay green
Human beings keep spilling out pollution
We have to come to a solution
When we walk and run it is hard to breathe
All the toxins in the air just have to leave
I speak this message for the next generation
We must do something to save our nation
Our world is precious and is the only one we have got
The seasons are changing and winters are hot
I hope to say this loud and clear
Earth is our world
Round and pure
Destruction is a disease
Let us find its cure.

Archie Spencer (12)
Bexhill Academy, Bexhill-On-Sea

My Happiness

What is your happiness?
What can it be?
Playing with friends
Sometimes I don't like it to end
My happiness is lots of things
Games on the console
To endless dreams
To eating cheese and beans
Watching and playing football
Scoring a goal
Then Mum saying I'm on a roll!

I smile when I'm happy
I smile when I'm nervous
Sometimes you don't see below the surface
Joy is happiness like no other
Laughing and splashing in the swimming pool
Dancing and playing in bubbles
Fun in the sun
Sea and sand
Holding a bucket in the palm of my hand
What is your happiness?
Is it just like me?
It's being all together
Happy as can be
With my friends and family!

Curtis Lawrence (12)
Forest Oak School, Smiths Wood

Buff People And Muscles

A kennings poem

Muscles trainer
Abs trainer
Biceps lover
Abdominal trainer
Big legs lover
Chizzled jaw lover
Stepping scales lover
Treadmill lover
Bench press-ups lover
Push-ups doer
Protein drinker
Gum chewer.

Brandon Evans (13)
Forest Oak School, Smiths Wood

All About Football

In this game you are a goal scorer
And a goal saver
You can defend the ball against ball skillers
You can clear the ball
You can be a ball clearer
If you are dedicated
You can be a dedicated football player.

Isaac Golby (14)
Forest Oak School, Smiths Wood

Lord Of The Rings

A kennings poem

Ring maker
Beast slayer
Dragon rider
Demon killer
Blade welder
Shadow hunter
Orc finder
Ring destroyer
Army leader
Magic caster
Eye killer.

Daniel Bladon (13)
Forest Oak School, Smiths Wood

The Hobbit

A kennings poem

Adventure joiner
Company leader
Dragon hunter
Hobbit finder
Orc killer
Book writer
Key finder
Dragon eyer
Mountain eyer.

Georgina Evans (14)

Forest Oak School, Smiths Wood

Nintendo Switch Gamer

My electric charger has given my game power
I can play Victory Royale
I can play lots of games
I can use my zombie maker.

Evan Mcintosh (13)
Forest Oak School, Smiths Wood

Henry The Vacuum Cleaner

A kennings poem

Room cleaner
Fast mover
Happy racer
Red sucker
Long piper
Dirt remover
Best friender
Mess destroyer.

Harley Morris (13)
Forest Oak School, Smiths Wood

Things You Need To Know About The PlayStation

A kennings poem

Money waster
Time eater
Fun bringer
Rage maker
Argument maker
Friend maker.

O'Shay Woolley (13)
Forest Oak School, Smiths Wood

The Bermuda Triangle

A kennings poem

Ship stealer
Fear bringer
Compass breaker
News hitter
Plane crasher.

Rhys Bolton (14)

Forest Oak School, Smiths Wood

About Me

A kennings poem

Maths lover
Play gamer
Dog lover
Pasta hater.

Keegan Bird (13)
Forest Oak School, Smiths Wood

The Protester

The clear blue seas... delightful
The smiling sun... alluring
The fully-grown trees... divine
The ocean air... exquisite

Golden sand brushing through my fingers
Content animals free to roam
Spotless landscapes, alongside rich and succulent grass
Whoosh! Whoosh!

But then things come into focus
The waves from my pillow hug my ears
Beep! Beep! Beep!
My feet dart to the side of my bed
The alarm finally stops

Plastic bags fly past my window
Fumes chug out of passing cars
Trees get chopped down by the second
What's happened to the world?

Turtles get coaxed into nets
Glass gets dumped onto the streets
Polluted air merrily enters our lungs
But it's time to fight back!

Ruby Turp (11)
Hassenbrook Academy, Stanford-Le-Hope

Save Our World!

Where has the world gone?
Where is the peace and friendliness?
Now it is all pollution and war.
Where is the beautiful world?
Where is all the nature and trees everywhere?
Now it's all destruction.
All the animals are fading away because they have
no home.
Where has the fun in life gone?
When will it reappear?
The questions can be answered
If everyone stops to catch some nostalgia.
With the breath of life we can reverse our ways
To find peace and beauty
With no wars and crimes.
How about we try this today?
Stop destruction and save our world.
Save our animals
And save our world!

Leo Dormer (12)
Hassenbrook Academy, Stanford-Le-Hope

A Protest Against Climate Change

People are against people owning petrol cars;
Others moan about fossil fuels and factories.
Most of them protest
But that doesn't help.
Protesters stick themselves to roads,
Some hang on bridges.
This is just causing traffic on the roads,
Also making cars stay idle.
This means that more fumes are floating in the atmosphere.
Humans can't enjoy their lives anymore,
Just because of climate change.
But there is one more thing I'm angry about:
Deforestation!
You're killing animals and that's not right.
But I'm not going to protest
Because I am that bright.

Samuel Clark (11)
Hassenbrook Academy, Stanford-Le-Hope

Fight For Our Future

The grass is brown
The air is dirty
Animals are going extinct
The trees are going
We're struggling to breathe
It used to be heaven
But now it's hell
2023 might not be good
But 2019 was beautiful
Let's save our planet
Get rid of the devil
Bring back the angel
If we don't stop this mess we will become extinct too!
Factories don't help, nor do buildings
Change having a car to not having a car
Earth is crying out so why won't anyone help?
If we don't stop this now there will be no one left to save
Because we will all be gone!

Jessica Patch (11)
Hassenbrook Academy, Stanford-Le-Hope

There's Still Hope

Plastic, death, extinction, the end:
Love, happiness, kindness, hope,
If only we could see what we'll surely soon approach,
If only this could be our last worry,
Unfortunately many think there is no hurry,
Many animals have already become extinct -
The past now in their name.

But they are not the only ones affected...
The oceans cry their helpless tears,
Pleading, praying, desperate,
For someone just to hear,
Don't let the past repeat itself,
Now it's up to you,
To help us to allow the planet to power through.

Elliote Watson-White (12)
Hassenbrook Academy, Stanford-Le-Hope

Change

I believe we can change the world
Change this mess that's in a swirl
Animals are being hurt
And plants are dying in the dirt
The oceans are dried out like dust
Everyone is listening to the government we can't trust
Every day I'm trapped in a cycle that never ends
We are ruining the Earth
We soon will have no sea to surf
The weather is getting worse day by day
If we don't help, children won't be able to go outside and
play
Let's help change the world so it can be as good as a pearl.

Emmanuela Koin (11)

Hassenbrook Academy, Stanford-Le-Hope

How To Help Save The World

G iant forests get pulled down
L ots of animals get killed
O f course, not many people care
B ut we can take action
A nd save our Earth
L ittle things are big things

W hen you have finished something... recycle
A nd turn your appliances off
R unning water should be shut off
M aybe try cutting back on car journeys
I do all these things
N ow maybe you should try
G reat things will happen if you do these.

George Darrah (11)
Hassenbrook Academy, Stanford-Le-Hope

Climate Change

C an we change the things we did?
L ike how we broke the ozone?
I f that can be possible, so can anything
M aybe we need to give it a try
A ct on changing animals' lives
T here is no Planet B
E ven if we try

C an you help us fight for our planet?
H ave a think about it
A fter all, you can help in many ways
N othing is impossible
G ive it a chance
E ven if that means doing the bare minimum.

Mary-Jane White (12)
Hassenbrook Academy, Stanford-Le-Hope

The Waves

The waves crash against the rocks,
The waves crash against the sand,
Filled with wonders,
They wash up on land,
The waves crash into the caves,
Weak and brave,
Filled with dirt and horror,
They fly away,
The waves swaying onto the sand,
Magical and strong,
Filled with wonders,
They wash up on land,
And the waves then bring joy,
As the waves are soon to be clean,
The dirt is gone,
The waves.

Maya Smith (12)
Hassenbrook Academy, Stanford-Le-Hope

Help Our Planet!

C hange is necessary
L ove is key
I will stand with you
M ake use of yourself and help
A ll of us should stand up for our world
T reat our planet better
E arth needs to be cared for

C an you help?
H ave a think and change
A ct now with us
N ever stop helping
G ood people equals a healthy Earth
E arth needs our help!

Ruby Dear (12)
Hassenbrook Academy, Stanford-Le-Hope

How Should We Change Climate Change?

How did climate change get here?
It's freaking us out
Oh no, we should run away
We could research it
Or maybe go back to find out what's happening
We could die because of climate change
It is deadly
Maybe we should just go home and look it up on the internet
It's scary
We could die
We could get lucky and survive
But we could get killed in the future if we walk out without our gas masks!

Daisy Bennett (11) & Lily
Hassenbrook Academy, Stanford-Le-Hope

Climate Change

C hanging the Earth
L ying, saying it's okay
I n our minds
M oney is everything
A nd no one cares about the future
T imes are changing
E vermore, it's terrifying

C hanging our future
H oping we can fix it
A nd now it's too late
N ow our Earth is doomed
G rowth is ending
E nding way too soon.

Imogen Reynolds (11)
Hassenbrook Academy, Stanford-Le-Hope

Polluted Atmosphere

Pollution
A devastating action
It is too late
It is horrific
Let's stop it before it is too late

Pollution
Deadly to every animal including us
It's as bad as saying a cuss
Let's stop it and change our world
Before we see it all swirled

Pollution
Crippling our environment
This is not what we meant
Let us change our ways
Before we run out of days.

Elliot Hodgins (12)
Hassenbrook Academy, Stanford-Le-Hope

The Rising Waters

The sea is rising higher,
the coasts are being flooded.
As it will be higher than the islands,
swallowing them whole.

When you're in the water,
the waves are in control.
The fish are flying to the skies,
the water's rising.

People are fleeing their homes,
because the water is rising loads.
In a couple of decades you know
the water will have risen you know.

George Durden (11)
Hassenbrook Academy, Stanford-Le-Hope

Climate Change

C hange is needed
L ove our environment
I know you can help
M ake use of your rubbish - recycle!
A ll of us need to work together
T ogether we can help the world
E arth needs us!

C ome and help
H appy Earth, happy us
A ct now!
N ever give up on your Earth
G o out and help
E arth needs us!

Keziah Gill (11)

Hassenbrook Academy, Stanford-Le-Hope

Oh How I Miss The Earth...

Oh how I miss the damp petrichor smell after the heavy rain.
Oh how I miss the crystal-clear blue seas.
Oh how I miss the wild and free animals.
Oh how I miss the vivid dreams of a healthy Earth which was cared for.
I miss the old meaning of Earth.
The old Earth.
The Earth that we cared so much for and now so little.
Our planet, Earth, I miss you.
I miss you very much!

Alisha Akther (12)
Hassenbrook Academy, Stanford-Le-Hope

I Remember...

I remember the day the world began to heat.
I remember there was barely enough to eat.
I remember when the ice broke.
I remember when no one took action or spoke.
I remember when they came to save me.
They saved my home: the sea.
I remember when someone spoke.
The silenced curse suddenly broke.
I remember when the world cared...
And my habitat was spared.

Scarlett-Rose Baffour-Asare (12)
Hassenbrook Academy, Stanford-Le-Hope

Stop Now!

The sun is smiling
Sky is blue
Seas are divine
Soft grass under my feet
But everything changes
Boom! Boom!

The sun is too hot
It's our fault
The sky is grey
Filled with smoke
Seas are full of plastic
Everything is now tragic
The grass is dead
The trees have been chopped
This needs to stop!

Nya Jones (11)
Hassenbrook Academy, Stanford-Le-Hope

Save The Planet Earth

Save the planet Earth
it is dying from pollution and heating
do you know what it is worth?
Earth is falling apart, the world that we live in will be gone
babies won't be able to live a good life
when they grow up walking around their neighbourhood
with rubbish everywhere and trees all falling down
please, please save this planet!

Harry Spenceley (12)
Hassenbrook Academy, Stanford-Le-Hope

Climate Change

It's our fault that the world is heating up
It's our fault that the trees are dying
It's our fault that climate change is going up
It's our fault because we are not looking after our homes,
places and workspaces
All countries need to make sure to clean up their spaces
We need to keep the world clean!

Triston Shaw (12)
Hassenbrook Academy, Stanford-Le-Hope

A Squirrel's Poem

Beautiful trees surround us,
Birds fly all around us,
An ocean of ice,
Flowers smell nice,
Oh no, the humans have found us!

Horrible cars pollute the Earth,
Watch as they invade our turf,
They cut down trees
And take all the leaves,
Please stop destroying our Earth!

Jack Hawkins (11)
Hassenbrook Academy, Stanford-Le-Hope

The World

I believe we can save the planet
just if we can plan it
if we use our words loud and clear
there might not be as much beer
we can't stay quiet and just shed a tear
while the polar bears die in fear
the fact is we're ruining our world
but we can fix it with just one word.

Ethan Cheeseman (12)
Hassenbrook Academy, Stanford-Le-Hope

Pollution Stop

Save, save, save the trees,
Save the polar bears and all the other endangered species,
Ice caps melting every day,
Soon they will all go away,
Air pollution stop,
Plastic pollution stop,
Eco-friendly is on top but deforestation is not!

Rio Hudson (11)
Hassenbrook Academy, Stanford-Le-Hope

Climate Change Today

Climate change
Year by year
We can do something
If we cheer
This Earth
Could almost look like a Smurf
As the sun shines bright
But it isn't fun tonight
Animals dying every day
Climate change
Needs to end today.

Mason Down (11)
Hassenbrook Academy, Stanford-Le-Hope

We Can Be Better

I believe that we can be better
stop writing as many letters
as with every letter we write a tree is cut down
and the sun warms up and the polar bears frown
lots of pollution is in the sea
many animals becoming extinct like the bees.

Jazmine Mason (12)
Hassenbrook Academy, Stanford-Le-Hope

My Poem

Changing through time
And space also suffering
Burning our Earth
We are doomed for the future
The future's being sold
Monstrosities are coming
Tired and cold words
Do not hurt us
But actions can we are told.

Alex Huggett (12)
Hassenbrook Academy, Stanford-Le-Hope

Save The Planet

How could this world be so cruel?
Don't forget the fossil fuels,
Big or small,
It's affecting them all
And affecting you too,
Teach your children about the sun
And let them know what it's done.

Hollie Firth (12)
Hassenbrook Academy, Stanford-Le-Hope

Revival

The past
So beautiful
Natural and full of life
But then us humans came and
We made the future dimmer
Soon the world will die
Just because of our sins
Unless we reform
Making a revival!

Alfie Drew (11)
Hassenbrook Academy, Stanford-Le-Hope

Dead Earth

The Earth is in need,
And we can help,
So come,
Please,
We can all work together!
To help this fallen world,
And make it great again.

Hannah Smallbone (11)
Hassenbrook Academy, Stanford-Le-Hope

Time For Change

A haiku

Climate change is bad
Seas and forests are at risk
The world needs to change.

Leo Brown (11)
Hassenbrook Academy, Stanford-Le-Hope

Save Our World
A haiku

Climate change is bad
It is not good for our world
Today we can change.

Murray Nifton (11)
Hassenbrook Academy, Stanford-Le-Hope

Now Or Never!

What is more splendid than the world itself and everything
the Earth gives you?
Majestic mountains,
Oceans of crystal blue,
Thundering skies,
Hues of weird and wonderful colours,
Rivers of undetected underground,
Streams beloved and untamed,
Majestic views of alluring landscapes,
Animals of all kinds,
Plants of great arrays of colours and shapes,
Uplands and wetlands,
Sun-dappled meadows,
Flourishing forests too,
Everything the Earth gives you!
Now the burning question is: what are we going to do?
There is no time to waste, the world we live in is at stake.
No longer majestic mountains, instead colossal piles of
ruins,
No longer oceans of crystal blue but piles of plastic filling
the waters
Waters that once filled the Earth's crevices!
No longer thunderous skies but an endless pit of jet black
surrounding the Earth of what used to be,
No longer hues of colours, no life to be seen,
No longer rivers running rapid, more like endless ventures of
untouched land utterly dried up,

No sign of water to ever touch the gravel of the once Earth
No longer views of gold, no longer landscapes showing us
its rare beauty to any astonished viewer!
No longer animals thriving: all extinct, long gone from forest
floors,
No longer plants growing in every field, now turned into
endless deserts,
No longer sun-dappled meadows,
No longer flourishing forests too,
Everything the world gave to you, gone!
So let me ask you: what are we going to do?
It's now or never to clean up the mess we've made
The damage we've caused already,
There's still time to fix this,
It's now or never!

Connie Mason (12)
Hethersett Academy, Hethersett

The Battlefield

Through the chaos of the battlefield, I see...
Orange and red scales shining in the sun, reflecting in my eyes.
Teeth showing from its mouth, wanting everyone to know it can bite,
I stand statue-like, my soldiers looking at me in fear and fright.
The demon's claws imprinting the ground, preparing to destroy,
Looking at me dead in the eye, I stare as it steps closer.
My heartbeat gradually getting faster, feeling it will pop out of my body,
The spikes on the beast's back point up like it will detach from its back.
Nostrils flaring up and down, ready for attack,
Fire creeping out from its mouth, spreading all around us.
Its heat melting my armour, shield and weaponry dripping onto my boots,
The smell of blood shifts from the unliving warriors to my nose, making it twitch.
A cacophony of screams flows into my ears, forming a tear that rolls down my cheek,
Flames from the fire mirror into my eyes as the creature gets nearer.
Its red eyes glowing into my soul, waiting and watching,
Wings floating higher and higher into the air, creating a gust of wind as it flies into the sky.

Olivia Emms (11)
Hethersett Academy, Hethersett

Our Future

No one believes us because we are young,
But we will not stop until this battle is won.
Our future is stolen and we are the thieves,
The list goes on and on of endangered species
Whilst we're pumping pollutants into the air,
Our world is dying and this isn't fair.
The sea levels are rising and flooding the land,
Temperatures are flying and getting out of hand.
Don't cry to me when your child has to imagine what a rhino
is 'cause they're extinct!
Don't come to me when the forests are gone,
I will just tell you to look at the things we did wrong.
We finally see the droughts and floods but still won't accept
it's our problem to fix,
For the endangered list is now more than 16,306.
Dear future generations to come,
I hope you realise what we have done,
We've thrown our world away
But people in charge will do nothing to repay
The creatures that were here before,
The ones we may see no more.

Verity Hamilton (12)
Hethersett Academy, Hethersett

Music

Listening to it, closing your eyes.
Imagining yourself on top of a building in New York,
Lights everywhere, in a crowd at a concert, nature
everywhere.
It's a safe place, a getaway.
It's an inspiration, a personality.
It helps define who you are.

I listen as I write; picking words from each verse or chorus.
All constructed perfectly to display a message of sorrow, of
joy, of complication, of desire.
'You', 'here', 'curiosity', 'dreams'.
Already a poem, each song flows.
Music has many genres, all of which connect to an emotion,
an identity.
Electric, pop, rock,
Harsh, soft, meaningful.

Music is more than words or rhythm,
To focus on these words: you find a message.
A message that connects you to your feelings, that helps,
that encourages.
It helps you find yourself - when everything's twisted.
It's me. It's what makes the question 'sight or hearing'
impossible.

It's what makes me cry most.
What makes me speechless...

It's music.

Emily Wilkinson (13)
Hethersett Academy, Hethersett

Swim Or Drown

For my life I will swim,
for swimming I'll give my life,
when I'm in the water I can't breathe,
but I am free,
when I'm on land I can breathe,
my mind goes to a place of its own,
but it doesn't feel alone,
with I am sane,
without I feel insane,
but I'm not free,

Up on the block,
you hear the water's heart pounding,
everyone else's voice tries to cancel yours out,
just breathe,
in and out,
everything stops,
then the beep,
harder than ever,
I push my body passed its limits,

Push too hard and I will drown,
don't push hard enough and I won't be proud,
wake up early,
go to bed late,
put in the work,

I don't care if I break,
I just need to win,
not just a gold medal,
but my dream,
I need to focus,
or I will drown,
not by water,
not by holding my breath,
not by pushing too hard,
but by my disappointment and anger.
I need to swim or I will drown.

Hollie Gilbertson (13)
Hethersett Academy, Hethersett

Skiing

Driving with skis in the back of the car,
Knowing it won't be far.
I can see them,
The mountains with snow piled on top.
Finally, the car makes a stop,
I can see them clearly,
I can see a new adventure.

Top of the mountain,
Top of the world,
Peering down at the view
And it doesn't scare me or you.

I can see it all,
I can see everything.
I feel like a cloud,
Or maybe the sun.
I feel like a butterfly,
Flying for fun.

Skiing down I notice a tree,
It looks like it is looking at me.
People in front swirling and twirling,
I start carving and whirling.
Losing control I crash into a tree,
Everybody looking at me.

I look here and there, I still don't care,
I pick up my skis and fly through the air,
The snow is blowing on my face,
It's a 'me vs the world' race.
I know the track,
From my hand to back,
Finishing in record time,
The bells start to chime.

Katherine Foster (12)
Hethersett Academy, Hethersett

My Place, My Home

Laving my house once more, escaping the grasp of
these walls.
Walking down the street, listening to music
To my favourite place to spend my time, the fields.
Walking past everything I've ever known
To be alone.
A safe time to think about my responsibilities and actions
A lead into reality.
Walking past the horses I once knew and the sheep
I love to walk, forever walking.
Thinking about my childhood, replaying it.
Watching my tree fall down to pieces and rot,
My tree all gone.
Reminiscing it, sitting on it, reliving my childhood.
Sword fighting the air, I'm finally home.
Lying down in the fields, on branches, having the best time
of my life
My home, my place.
Hills and holes growing and growing.
Branches twirling and twisting around my memories.
Been three years since it was first found,
Oh how good it was leaving my house
Once more escaping the grasp of these walls.

Emilia Wright (12)
Hethersett Academy, Hethersett

Little Magpie

Little magpie, little magpie so majestic and sweet.
A little bird that sweeps along the land.
Flittering and fluttering to its own accord.
Searching for shiny gold and dazzling silver.
Little magpie, little magpie so majestic and sweet.
The freshly formed dew of the morning sun.
Glistening with the rays of the shining sun.
When the summer turns to winter the little magpie builds
a nest.
Little magpie, little magpie so majestic and sweet.
One for sorrow, two for joy, three for a girl and four for
a boy.
Five for bronze, six for silver, seven for gold and eight
for platinum.
Little magpie, little magpie so majestic and sweet.
Flittering and fluttering until it falls asleep.
Little magpie, little magpie so majestic and sweet.
Searching for gold and silver till the snow turns to sleet.

Maisie Buckle (11)
Hethersett Academy, Hethersett

Ode To Cheese

There once was a man called Bob
Who liked to stuff cheese in his gob
He ate his car keys
Along with some cheese
And walked to work with a sob.

So he ended up arriving at work late
Only getting there at half-past eight
And he told his boss
Who was very cross
That he had been hit around the head with a plate.

Bob worked as a cheese taster in a cellar
Trying Wensleydale, Parmesan and Cheddar
He ate cheese through the night
And ate cheese on a flight
And tried hard to eat cheese whenever.

By the end of the day he was full of cheese
Since in this field he had such great expertise
And he felt so inspired
But also very tired
And so he tumbled and fell to his knees.

Bob spent the rest of his prosperous life
With Cheddar galore and little strife

And so that is why
You should buy
Cheese for a long and joyful life!

Luke Hood (12)
Hethersett Academy, Hethersett

Life On The Court

Basketball, the beautiful game,
It could even be your train to fame,
But when I play I'm at the top of my key,
I'm always moving and grooving,
Crisscrossing and bossing
And my skills will leave you
Sliding, diving and riding to the floor,
Yeah because my skills are ankle breaking
And to finish... a ferocious finger roll,
Swish! Straight in the hole!
You see, my game's so acclaimed,
So outright dirty it will put you to shame,
I'm aflame and everyone knows my name,
When I open fire, I inspire,
The hoop's for sale and I'm the buyer,
Like a bolt of lightning, I'm sizzling,
Tonight I'm delivering,
That's how I like to be dribbling,
But at the end of the game, you bet when I shoot it's all net!

Adnan Elzubeir (12)
Hethersett Academy, Hethersett

As Much As I Dreamed, As Much As I Had

As much as I dreamed, as much as I had
I could not help but think back to what was before
I always like to say that it is not that bad
But indeed I cannot forget what I saw
As the temperature increases
The health of our planet decreases
It's too late to stop it now, even with pretty pleases
As time goes on they say the pain eases
But seeing our planet in this state, how could I sit still?
Just thinking about it makes me feel ill
They say don't think of the past, it will do you no good
But what if the past did better than the future ever could?

But as much as I dreamed, as much as I had
I could not help but think back to what was before
Where nature flourished and thrived
And plastic didn't wash up on the seashore.

Rama Hamad (12)
Hethersett Academy, Hethersett

Earth... Our Choice!

Upon the marble globe, we live,
Studded with jewels, green and blue,
It's stunning, full of human spirit,
The only one, true and pure.
Mountains, rivers, grasslands and reefs,
Dwellings, habitats, wilderness too,
Volcanoes burst with their dragon's breath,
Sweltering sulfur and smoke they spew.
Upon the marbled globe, we live,
The ice is gone, their home perished,
Seeing the polar bears go extinct,
Our planet left bare and human ego flourished.
Barren and bald lay land deforested,
Dry as a desert, it's the price we pay,
Jungles, savannahs, many gone and uprooted,
Coasts crumble and new boundaries lay.

Oh no! Not the inky, smelly destiny we foresee,
The power is ours to keep the world crystal clean.

Pranati Shastri (11)
Hethersett Academy, Hethersett

Family Forever

My family tree will forever keep growing,
For a good family will provide love to keep it flowing.
I love everyone in my family,
We all get along with each other happily.
I love my muma, pop, aunties and uncles,
I love my grandad, granny, my sister and my pets.
I love my great-grandad and those that are up above.
I don't know what I would do without any of you because
you are always by my side,
Even when I want to crawl up into a ball and hide.
Family is caring, sharing, calming, no harming and helping
when you are yelping.
Families are polite and listen while you share bad news.
Family is not something that you get to choose,
They come to you when you are confused.
You only get one family and that family is forever.

Maisie Powles-Warren (11)
Hethersett Academy, Hethersett

Every Good Has A Bit Of Bad

Walking across the battlefield completely zoned out,
All I could hear was the faint screams of agony.
I couldn't hold my head up,
But looking down was even worse!
It was like a mountain of the deceased.
As I stared at the corpses
I couldn't help but fall to my knees and cry.

While sobbing into my knees,
My friend ran up to me and held me...
I was glad to have this as one of my last memories
I took one last look around and thought, *what have I done?*
All I could do was grab a gun
Hold it to my head and pull the trigger.
Suddenly it all went black
The last thing I could remember was a voice saying,
"You ended it too early and now it's too late..."

Max Bagge (11)
Hethersett Academy, Hethersett

I Am A Swimmer

I am a swimmer.
Early morning training in the pitch-black cold,
My shivering in the pool has become uncontrolled.
I am a swimmer.
Endless laps, gaining strength in mind and body with each one,
Knowing that the dedication to pain has not yet begun.
I am a swimmer.
The sound of panting, as breathless as a dog, is loudly heard,
Knowing the next competition will be flawless and undeterred,
I am a swimmer.
As race day approaches, I begin the gruelling and exhausting sets,
To minimise my effort in order for progress.
I am a swimmer.
Race day is here and I'm behind the blocks,
I know I'm ready.
I am a swimmer and here is my hard work leading to success!

Sofia Stosic (12)
Hethersett Academy, Hethersett

A New Day

The sun rises, it's a new day,
Time to wake up for a new adventure,
The sun hides behind gloomy clouds,
The leaves blow past in the winter wind
It's a new day and a new adventure
Time to devise a plan to find the treasure
The treasure was a once-a-year paradise
Waiting and waiting, enduring through winter
Finally the treasure in my eyes
The sun shines on the glistening waters
But it shortly goes away
No worries, here comes autumn, just right
But that shortly passes and it becomes cold and dark
The cold winter comes back but winter is not all bitter
At least there is Christmas
And soon a new year and a new day
And a new treasure to discover.

Keyaan Ahmed (12)
Hethersett Academy, Hethersett

Fly Again

Guns, mortars, shells and tanks
Help me, God, and help our souls
As thy shells whip and whine
With a power so divine
I hear the cries and hear the bang
Rippling and tearing through the wind
We fight back but we are weak
But we will not be meek
We will fight to the end
But mourn the dead
We are bound together
With fear and terror
We will take back our country
No price too high, no mercy to be shown
We will take on our nemesis one by one
And burn their souls in Hell
We'll walk a thousand miles
Take lives
And build our country again
We are not scared
We are not in fear
As we know our flag will fly again!

Zak Lawrenson (12)
Hethersett Academy, Hethersett

The Future!

My burning question is: why do we live in the past?
Everyone from my generation asks.
We have finally woken up and realised
The people promoting global warming actions
Were all in disguise
The people working hard hard
Will never have a nice house and backyard
It's all about authority
The majority of the government will get applause for their
small undiscoverable contribution
The effort that goes unnoticed is always the most impactful
I can't see a future or clear peace
Don't blame me for being in denial
The change one person can make in their life can be
important
My burning question is: why do we live in the past?

Harriet Dingle (12)
Hethersett Academy, Hethersett

Self-Consciousness

Why do people get so worked up
About things that don't matter?
Like height, weight, facial features
And their life altogether?
Why do people look across the room,
Burning with green-eyed envy?
You are the way you are
And are beautiful in many ways.
Why does it matter
If we are shorter than our friends?
We are all different people
And that's not going to change.
Why are we never good enough
To meet our expectations?
We are too fat, too short or not good enough for
our friends.
You are fine the way you are.
So please don't worry,
You are perfect already
And don't need to be changed.

Zoë Menegaz MacLean (12)
Hethersett Academy, Hethersett

What Are We?

Passion. The thing that makes us human.
Our drive to succeed,
Our hopes and dreams,
The things we must desire,
Like a burning fire rising inside of us.
The thrill of success;
Our thoughts, feelings and determination.
They are the reasons we are who we are.
A world without passion is pointless,
Not caring, not wishing, not questioning.
We wouldn't feel anything,
Not even anger or sadness.
No, we only feel rage because we care,
We only understand heartbreak because we believe in love.
Passion isn't just wanting things to happen.
Passion is us.
Passion.
It's the thing that makes us human.

Charlie Ward (12)
Hethersett Academy, Hethersett

Monkeh

Monkeh had started his game of tag
To prove himself and place his flag
A monkey by the name of Cheese
Chased him up the side of a nearby tree
He looked as if he was covered in molten lava
This was going to cause some drama
Top Hat Monkey ran across the wall
As if it was late in the mall
The ground which was covered in snow
Made a crunch as he fell
Bob the snowman was looking at him
Because Monkeh had gone to the gym
He branched his way to the platforms
To go to the treehouse in the warm
Suddenly Top Hat Monkey came out of nowhere
Like a grizzly bear
Monkey got tagged
It started again
Monkeh!

Jacob Farrow (12)
Hethersett Academy, Hethersett

Glorious Horses

The glorious things you can do,
With your own horse, except mucking out poo!
Like brushing your equine,
Until he sparkles and shines,
Getting him splashed,
Until he's painted and washed,
Jumping over some poles,
Making sure we reach our goals,
Riding around the dressage arena,
Just like a ballerina,
Checking everything is clean for a photo shoot,
Even the tip of your riding boot,
Dressing up to go out and about,
Not worrying about all the shout,
If your horse does a buck,
You better sit up,
Oh, the glorious things you can do,
With your very own horse, except mucking out poo!

Mia Maklakov (12)
Hethersett Academy, Hethersett

The Game Of Football

So there is this game that's called football,
If you haven't heard of it, don't fret,
While you're playing, you might take a fall,
But you should hit the ball into the net,
There are pros who can hit it really hard,
Though it might be saved due to a goalkeeper,
Then there are defenders who try to guard,
I'm sure Messi is the best footballer,
The person in charge is the referee,
They oversee the players and the match,
Then the goal protector is the goalie,
And they might make an amazing catch,
There are also sports that you can play indoors,
But the best is football for evermore!

Leo Beurich (13)
Hethersett Academy, Hethersett

Hope

Flowing fields of flourishing flowers,
Rolling rivers rich in rainbow,
Elegant efflorescences of eupatoriums,
Towering trees tangled in twisters,
Wondrous wildlife wandering free,
A world that needs preserving,
But darkness is soon to dominate,
Fathomless factories frothing with fog,
Lagoons of litter lethally layered,
Tons of trees tumbling to the turf,
But amongst the gloom, a glimmer of hope,
People playing their part in protecting the planet,
Boundless beauty worth battling for,
Time to take action before time runs out,
Hope is on the horizon.

Megan Banyard (11)
Hethersett Academy, Hethersett

Vulture

Vulture, vulture, soaring high
in the darkness of the sky
why are you designed to be
so powerful to creatures like you and me?

When you're soaring through the sky
are you happy to see animals die?
How many carcasses are you going to eat
before you are swept off your feet?

Do you come out at night or day?
People would want to throw you away
your laser eyes
make people say their goodbyes

Vulture, vulture, soaring high
in the darkness of the sky
why are you designed to be
so powerful to creatures like you and me?

Jake Ansbro (11)
Hethersett Academy, Hethersett

First Day Of School

It's my first day of school,
Don't know what to do,
Don't know where to go,

Stressed in the playground corner,
All alone and cold,
What should I do?
It's only my first day of school.

Class after class,
No one to talk to.
I'm so stressed out!
Oh, what should I do?
It's only my first day of school.

Sat alone during lunch,
When someone comes to me
And they ask,
"Can I sit here?"
Could this be my first friend?

No longer alone,
One person can change your world!

Gabriela Kachoviciute (12)
Hethersett Academy, Hethersett

Summer

Summer, summer shining bright
As it illuminates the sky above.

As the wind whistles through the vibrant green leaves
You can feel the sun on your face
Beaming through the gaps of the summer tree.

Summer, summer shining bright
As it illuminates the sky above.

As I sit against the tree I can hear the imperfect waves
In front of me and rushing against the sand.

Summer, summer shining bright
As it illuminates the sky above.

As I lay down to rest my eyes
I can hear the birds singing and tweeting in the sky above.

Neve Williams (11)
Hethersett Academy, Hethersett

The Ancient Buildings

Ancient buildings, who remembers them?
Who remembers their names?
Who remembers their times?
Who remembers their stories?
The stories told?
The stories that lived?
The stories that fell?
The stories that stayed?

The love for these buildings was so majestic,
People's hearts used to melt for them till the dusk of day,
The night flowed with the stars above,
Cascading, submerging the sky until day's dawn.
Their beauty was great, glorifying is all it would do,
While waiting for the moment, for it to say, "I miss you!"

Eva Haddon (12)
Hethersett Academy, Hethersett

Don't Give In

They may think it's okay to call me names,
punch me, kick me
or burn my textbook to flames.
But I truly do not give in
to the horrible mistreatment
that makes my head spin.
Even online they put me through
the terrible torture - it grew and grew.
After some time
the bullying stopped,
the name-calling, the torment,
the fake personality dropped.
The heart in my chest
has been repaired and fixed,
I truly have been blessed
with my family who didn't let this persist.

Willow Bradley (12)
Hethersett Academy, Hethersett

Rubik's Cube

Just bought a perfect cube.
So excited.
Then scrambled, confused,
First time turning, click-clacking, rotating and twisting,
Scattering colours hurting my head.
Excited, rejected, stranded and abandoned,
Now a messed-up decoration on the shelf.
Time passes.
Then a spark, an idea, inspiration to make it right,
On one side, a white cross, the first small steps,
Getting somewhere?
Twisting and turning, click-clacking again.
Finally finished, as we began.

Frank Olson (12)
Hethersett Academy, Hethersett

A Good Day

When I wake up
I go and grab a cup
To make the perfect cup of tea
On my way to school I see the best tree
I see my best friend
Our friendship will never end
My first lesson is English
Then we finish
Now we have break
Now maths, I did not make a mistake
Once I get home
I search for something on Google Chrome
Google Classroom obviously!
Doing my homework consciously
That's the end of my day
And put my homework in I try!

Jacob Dye (11)
Hethersett Academy, Hethersett

The Internet

Are you okay?
Does it make you feel up high or down low?
Should you put it away and leave it alone?
There may be good, helpful or engaging,
But through everything, there must be something.
Scarring, scary or even traumatising,
Your 'for you page' is endless and it can make you feel
that way too!
Corners that are turned are unpredictable,
You can never know what the outcome will be.
It can be a dangerous place... the internet!

Erin Laughton (12)
Hethersett Academy, Hethersett

The Lesson

Birds calling, clock ticking, people laughing.
Why can't I just concentrate?

Thoughts of playing, programmes waiting, Xbox calling.
Please brain, just concentrate!

Tummy rumbling, lunch pending: sausage rolls, fizzy pop.
Please, please, just concentrate!

Peers distracting, talking and fiddling, name on the board.
Just concentrate!

Foot tapping, frustration rising, anger building,
Please just concentrate!

William Hale-Sutton (12)
Hethersett Academy, Hethersett

Overwhelming Thoughts

It was the day of the battle,
thoughts were crowding my head
All I could hear was an eerie silence
but in reality, it was all a scream
thoughts, overwhelming thoughts
As I walked further onto the battlefield
the mist rose from the ground
into my head and into my mind
The grass crunching underneath my feet
pulling me further and further
The realisation of my platoon around me
by my side
I was not alone!

Florence Parish (11)
Hethersett Academy, Hethersett

One Snowy Morning

One snowy morning, an ivy of white,
as well as a snowman just out of sight.
The hovering trees blow in the breeze,
as the glistening fountain is about to freeze.
The trees are like an archway covered in frost,
all sparkling and glistening but still somehow soft.
I walk through this wonderland,
forgetting all I have planned.
Just enjoying nature's miraculous treat,
at times like this my heart skips a beat!

Alice Russell (12)
Hethersett Academy, Hethersett

The Kindness Poem

I can choose to be kind
Each and every day I can choose to be kind
To everyone in every way
When I am kind to others I make the world a little brighter
When I am kind to others
I make my heart a little lighter
I pledge myself on this very day to try and be kind in
every way
To every person I can, big or small
I will help them if they fall
When I love myself and others too
That is the best I can do!

Harvey Bee (11)
Hethersett Academy, Hethersett

We Can Do This

We need to take responsibility for our world
Remember there is no Planet B
The Earth is getting warmer
The ice is melting, the polar bears are losing their homes
The oceans are getting polluted with our rubbish
We can stop this if we just...
Pick up the pieces of rubbish on the ground
Start burning less coal, oil and gas
Remember there is no Planet B
We can take responsibility for our world!

Poppy Fitzpatrick (11)
Hethersett Academy, Hethersett

Spring

As the sun delicately rose
The mountain peaks reflected the warm morning glow
All was silent as the baby animals awoke from their sleep
And the birds sang from high up in the trees
In the springtime mist, the vibrant blossoms swayed slowly in the breeze
There were butterflies, ladybirds, dragonflies and bees
They fluttered and frolicked until the sun set
And then all the animals went back to rest.

Liliana Clay (11)
Hethersett Academy, Hethersett

The Sea

Listen to the roaring waves
echoing around the caves
Deep, dark and mysterious
can be dangerous
The fish shimmer
and the water glimmers
The wind is mild
yet the sea is wild
The water is inviting
and the waves are very exciting
The bright blue
waves are see-through
The tide has a flow
while the ocean has a glow
The water is blue-green
and the view is serene.

Clementine Jacobson (12)
Hethersett Academy, Hethersett

The Seaside

Sand is everywhere
Between my toes
Between my fingers
And in my nose
Waves are crashing
Against stones and rocks
They make the sand wet
And the same with my socks
In the distance you can see
The sun shining bright
Above the sea
It sends a glow across the ocean
And illuminates the sky
It always makes you question
What you're seeing with your eye.

Oliver Wilson (11)
Hethersett Academy, Hethersett

A Boy With A Dream

He was only small
Smaller than all the others
He sometimes wondered why
But his dreams were big

Dreams of flying high
Way above the rim
Balls flying through the hoop
It may seem impossible
But not for him

It was like the court swallowed him
But that didn't stop him
His Jordans gave him wings
In truth, he was the boy with a dream.

Zach Ruiters (11)
Hethersett Academy, Hethersett

We Love Our Pets

It was time to say goodbye
And we knew we would cry
But life goes on and we needed to be strong
She was born a long way away
We travelled to say 'hey'
Tilly came back to her new home
Where she could grow and roam
Playing rough and tumble
The energy would rumble
Life is happy now we have our new friend
And we found our hearts could mend!

Georgia Blanch (12)
Hethersett Academy, Hethersett

Kindness

K indness should be all around
I nstead of hatred being found
N obody should ever feel sad
D oing things that make you mad
N ever feel that you are alone
E veryone should make their feelings known
S o always talk to someone you trust
S howing kindness is always a must.

Seth Ford (12)
Hethersett Academy, Hethersett

Self-Love

I sometimes see myself with pride,
Other times I hide or cry,
The mirror is no less than me,
Or what other people see,
I was not made to be perfect,
Nor was I made to be backswept,
I was not made to forget,
How to look at myself with kind eyes and warm concepts,
I was made to be real!

Ruby Cammack (12)
Hethersett Academy, Hethersett

Spring

Flowers are starting to grow
Birds start to sing
The wind will blow
Spring

Animals come out in sunlight
Birds flapping their wings
The sun blows bright
Spring

Lakes no longer frozen
What else could Mother Nature bring?
Rivers flowing in motion
Spring.

Alin Finaru (12)
Hethersett Academy, Hethersett

The Gymnast

Haiku poetry

Flexing and stretching
Conditioning, pointing toes
Making yourself warm

Gliding in the air
Swift, sprinting towards the vault
Tumbling with grace

It's time for cool down
Have I won a gold medal?
Rose cheeks, happy self.

Emily Lamb (11)
Hethersett Academy, Hethersett

Books

Hidden treasures,
Lost worlds,
Humbly majestic,
Imagination soaring,
Tales of old,
Sometimes,
Others not,
Heroes galore,
Villains and more,
Safely contained,
In humble binding,
For evermore,
Sealed in words.

Kitty Wilkins (13)
Hethersett Academy, Hethersett

Football

F un as you play
O pen to everyone
O fficial players
T hrilling teams
B est leagues
A udience booming chants
L ove for everyone
L oud audience.

Ben Hargrave (11)
Hethersett Academy, Hethersett

Together

Haiku poetry

Animals suffer
Sea levels rise and plants die
The Earth is warming

But all is not lost
We need to change our lifestyles
And we can fix this!

Together.

Aviv Chayut (12)
Hethersett Academy, Hethersett

Sausages

A haiku

Sausages are great
Their smell arouses senses
I can't wait 'til tea!

Thomas Brown (12)
Hethersett Academy, Hethersett

The Future Is In Your Hands

A haiku

I see your future
Its promise and its demise
Both lie in your hands.

Finley Bowyer (12)
Hethersett Academy, Hethersett

The Secret Of Chess

A game made about kings, by kings, for kings
But each player starts the same with the same rules
But how does that relate to life?
I have 8 pawns, 2 knights and 2 bishops
2 rooks, a king and a wife.

This game is all about betrayal and sacrifice
Practising your ruthlessness and cold heart
Exercising them like a virtuous quality society loudly
Cheers you to achieve once or twice
But forget to mention controlling our dark sides
Why should we ignore the dark?

The game has two lessons to preach
You need not a crown or a throne
To be king you need control, no one can escape your reach
You need the strength and skill but you need it to be known

A game also shows you the perspective of kings
A pawn only sees his friends on the battlefield and the
enemy on the other side
A king makes a circus out of their sacrifice using them
through invisible strings
But the king's enemies are over there and on his side

All games are fair, the only advantage is intelligence
and skill
The best ones end with a quick checkmate

And with a sharp sweet kill
Black A6, B7, C7, White... checkmate!

Ksawery Zylka-Zebracki (15)

Lincoln Castle Academy, Lincoln

Sentence

Crimson cruelty, bloodshed with hypocrisy,
The Devil's hands make an antagonist with puppetry,
Innocence murdered as the truth washes over me,
Manacles of trauma bind my wrists with insanity.

These demons bound to the victim weren't mine,
And my psychotic narcism just built over time,
Until I finally took those chances and I finally took that knife
And laid it at his diaphragm while screaming inside.

But there are two crowns in my psychotic chess game,
The hierarchy of Machiavellian lulls me all the same,
The torture he gave, the rules he disobeyed,
My captivating sentence mirrors their disdain.

Barely a soul at the funeral of mine
Kill the killer, a hypocrite is all you'll find,
Yet between angelic good and the wrong of his lies
A tyrannical victor of his own demise

And without his villainous ways, civility stood by him,
And it kills me to know my death was decided,
Yet if he was found out, there'd be no protracted trial,
So am I the antagonist or are they all in denial?

Evie Allen (13)
Lincoln Castle Academy, Lincoln

Seeing The Imperfections In Our Wonderful World

Accustomed to the lies that propaganda has encapsulated us within,
We turn a blind eye towards the significant plethora of imperfections in our so-called 'wonderful world'.
The robins flutter by in the midsummer sky,
Unbeknown to the absent-minded loggers just 100 metres away.
Their home is hacked, chopped and industrialised within a day,
Leaving other species in utter dismay.
Polar bears cry out on the other side of Earth as the ice caps melt,
Their utter desperation cannot be felt.
Hunting dominates the scene in many parts of Africa as elephants are just left to die,
All humans do is just sit there and sigh.
We're being intoxicated by our own gases being emitted,
Give it a few decades and oxygen will be an utter privilege.
However, we have many years to still turn this around yet,
Humanity can turn this round I bet!

Braeden Uzzell (13)
Lincoln Castle Academy, Lincoln

La Zenia

Oh beautiful La Zenia
A truly majestic place
It seems like nothing could go wrong in this Medittarrean paradise
The people though, I can't understand
I don't speak Spanish
But they are, let's say, nicer than here in Lincoln
Oh, must I forget about the food?
The food is absolutely delicious
The quality is amazing and that's just the food
The beachside view is just stunning
It almost seems like it's fake
The waves crashing onto the sandy surface
The palm trees waving as I go on the beach
The Spanish surface lights up as the sun wanders away from the starry sky.
The boats cruising on the breathtaking sea
They return to port and prepare for their next great day at beautiful La Zenia,
Oh beautiful La Zenia!

Ashton Maksymiw-Mullen (15)
Lincoln Castle Academy, Lincoln

My Sapphire Star

Distant, yet surroundings swarmed it
Shining brighter than anything else up there
Staring endlessly forever, never once left my sight
Already knowing this star wasn't going anywhere.

Mine to stare, care, listen and feel
To his gently gaze on me forever
His brightness outshone everyone in the room
He was never going to disappear, not ever

Enigmatic, luminous, there he stood alone
The brightest star I had ever seen
Giving me warmth without any physical contact
Even through my darkness, he continued to beam

Ocean-blue crystals and waves stared at me
Impossibly far away, unable to touch
Never mind the others that stood around him
He was the only star that mattered to me very much
My sapphire star.

Lucy Jones (14)
Lincoln Castle Academy, Lincoln

Mental Health Awareness

M ental health matters to everyone
E ventually people will realise how important it is
N o one should ever feel like they can't tell anyone
T he school can help you and let you talk about it
A nyone can suffer
L ittle girls and boys can be influenced by anything

H opefully there are people you can trust and tell
E ven if you don't want to tell anyone you should, no matter what
A nd if you won't get the help you need
L isten to people, they can offer advice and stuff
T ell people, make sure you can trust someone
H elp others in need, if something is going on.

Mia Sawyer (13)
Lincoln Castle Academy, Lincoln

The Beautiful Game Or The Game Of Corruption?

C orruption in FIFA is sadly very common

O perations were set to sabotage players, teams and countries

R eactions of the fans was depressing when uncovered

R ush of anger took the community as shown in interviews

U topia is what FIFA and the fans wanted until money came in

P artnerships with famous and powerful people made it worse

T ension between fans and FIFA arose as fights started

I ntentions were clear for FIFA as money was the only thing

O bsession with this took over the peaceful community

N ations were disrupted because of selfishness and millions were harmed to gain more numbers.

Mason Lunn (12)

Lincoln Castle Academy, Lincoln

Years Of Misery

Young to old,
We can't be bold.
Pain in and out,
It's the looks it's all about.

Lies and lies come out of them,
Feeling misery, it's everyone and then
The tension and anxiety increases
But my confidence and speech decreases.

The fear and fright of normal people,
I can't believe that bullying is legal.
I'm not sure if it's my personality or appearance
But the people around me need to help and make a
difference.
We use smiles to hide our feelings
But our depression and sadness are higher than the ceiling.
Some people can cope and cry
But others just tend to die.

Holly Law (13)
Lincoln Castle Academy, Lincoln

Until We Meet Again

I remember the moment clear as day
Sat there loving life
Who knew two words could ruin that?
'He's dead'.

Pain!

All sorts of emotions hitting me at once
Anger, heartache, sadness
Thinking what I could have done

Suddenly it hit me
He was gone
It was like nothing I have ever felt before

Emotions flying at me
"What have I done to deserve this?"
Tears rolling down my face
No pain had ever hit me like this before

You were loved by many
You had a long life ahead

Until we meet again...
Grandad.

Harvey Gleadhill (14)
Lincoln Castle Academy, Lincoln

The Future Of Our Planet

T rees are falling, animals are dying
H ere is a poem just for you
E arth needs you and you need Earth

F uture, future, soon to be with forests burning and animals losing their habitats but that is
U ntil now, now is when we change, for you it's finally time to change
T he planet is dying and children are crying because of the amount of pollution in the main cities
U nited Kingdom, USA Russia - everywhere needs you. This is
R eal! Polar bears are crying out on the cold melting part of the Earth but humans just sigh
E veryone, please help!

Oliver Lacey (12)

Lincoln Castle Academy, Lincoln

The Crimes Of Football

This may be a rhyme
But these fans are committing a crime
How can you want to do this
When all a player did was merely miss?
How can fans want this to stay?
Racism is not the right way
There is now corruption in this game
Does anyone feel the same?
These racist fans are ruining our game
Their slurs and chants attack the innocent
How can this be a famous game?
We can't have generations taking a glance
So watch the game and give them a chance
The world is so small
So rise tall
And help us defeat it
Racism should never win!

Brandon Thompson (12)
Lincoln Castle Academy, Lincoln

Do You Like The Ocean?

Do you like the ocean?
I do
It's a place with magnificent sealife
However, people take advantage of it
Our species of dolphins, there are only ten left?

I love the ocean
The gorgeous blue waves crashing against the shore
Rippling, rippling

It's a shame really
All of the pollution killing sea animals

Just a quick message from me to you
Next time you are walking with some rubbish
Find a bin
That's the home for your crisp packet
Not the water!

So,
Do you really like the ocean?

Jack Johnson (11)
Lincoln Castle Academy, Lincoln

Emotions

Emotions are something you can't control
You just have to roll with it 'cause there is no antidote
You can lock them in your room all safe and sound
Then scream into a pillow when there is no one around

Emotions are something you can't control
Don't beat yourself up, it's not your fault
People aren't blind
Don't fake your smile
Just say them out loud with no hesitation
No one will judge, we aren't all the same
We all have emotions but not on the same day.

Romina Rizaie (12)
Lincoln Castle Academy, Lincoln

Put Down That Game!

Why are you doing this?
While you are gaming
You should be out saving
The environment
It gives you air to breathe
It's time to remove deceiving news
Is it the end of the world?

While the trees are trying their hardest
We cut them down for useless tools
Why? Just why?
Come on, we have a world to fix
But it's not over yet
We have a chance to put things right

Are you going to join me or what?
Games are good and all
But you have better things to do!

Ethan Dimelow (12)
Lincoln Castle Academy, Lincoln

Be Yourself

Don't act upon other people's opinions.
Be yourself!
Don't let others define you.
It's your body, not theirs.
No one can have a perfect 'Barbie-like' figure.
It's not natural!
No matter how hard it gets, there is always someone to
talk to.
You are never alone.
Nobody should ever make you feel ashamed of yourself,
To the point where you have to turn to self-harm.
It will get better, I promise.
You are incredible so just be you because you are perfect.

Alice Bingham (12)
Lincoln Castle Academy, Lincoln

A Friend Who's There

I try to find,
What I cannot see,
When people aren't kind,
You're there with me.

When I struggle and fall,
And can't get back up,
You stop people making me feel small,
You're always the one to pull me up.

Others call me dramatic,
It's only you that sees,
You always make me ecstatic,
Thank you for being there with me.

I try to find,
What I cannot see,
But now I've found...
A friend who is always there for me.

Ella Woods (13)
Lincoln Castle Academy, Lincoln

A Future For The Forests

D o not let people ruin forests
E ven if you're not bothered
F or thousands of trees are being cut
O ver years trees won't exist
R ight now, trees are being cut
E ven if we need them to breathe
S o many animals are losing their habitats
T ogether we can save them
A nd
T o stop this from happening
I t could take
O ver a 100 years or possibly
N ever if we don't stop it now!

Evie Richardson (13)
Lincoln Castle Academy, Lincoln

It's Just Me

It used to be just us three
'Friends' we once said
Yet now they just ignore me
Act like I'm invisible instead

I ambled behind
As they strode ahead
I said I didn't mind
But I did in my head

Isolated and despondent
Never the first choice
Secluded and used
I had an unheard voice

But they will just never see
That it used to be just us three
A friendship that included me
But now it's just... me!

Imogen Woodhouse (14)
Lincoln Castle Academy, Lincoln

Save Our World

Having glossed over our fluffy carpets
Untold meat markets
Trained men, marksmen and the extinction of animals
worldwide
The greed of man has swept common life away
Greed has us taking lives for goods
If only blinded by want

Animals' lives exist but we seem to protest
We can change, right?
Treat the environment how you treat your pets or children
Treat the world like your child
It's irreplaceable and worth something more than money.

Lukasz Mehassouel (14)
Lincoln Castle Academy, Lincoln

Change

We need to make a change,
Our Earth is falling,
The ice is breaking,
Australia is burning,
Seasons are changing,
People are striking,
Kids are dying,
But...
There's no one helping,
No one's listening,
How can the dream turn into reality,?
Recycle properly,
Be kind to society,
Donate when you can,
Recycle, reuse and save our planet,
Mankind can make a difference,
Why not do it?
This is our responsibility.

Amy Laughton (14)
Lincoln Castle Academy, Lincoln

My Heated Heart

Today is the day we stop
Guys and girls, this is when we listen
Our nature is beginning to dissolve
Only some of us have followed our hearts
Below our pride the animals suffer
Life as we know it will be gone soon
Every tree and every animal will have gone too
This will be because of your actions
With death comes realisation
All of us will soon see.

Nicole Burrows (13)
Lincoln Castle Academy, Lincoln

Fanatic Football Fans

Fanatic football fans abuse fantastic footballers
Ravage racism ruins our worldwide game
Raheem receives racism all around our classless country
Many fans abuse him on and off the priceless pitches
Loud Lukaku luckily moved away from the fools and the
abuse they gave him and his family!

Reegan-Jay Wells (12)
Lincoln Castle Academy, Lincoln

Another Normal Day

It's another morning
Another day
Another breather
Another step
It's a usual boring day
I miss the old days
The walks on the dark, abandoned streets
The home-made food
The deep talks with the ones I trust the most
I miss it all!

Bianca Preda (13)
Lincoln Castle Academy, Lincoln

Words Bubble Up Like Soda Pop

Words bubble up like soda pop
Feels like I can't ever make them stop
Talking to you is like a dream
Feels like I'm disconnected from reality
Floating in space
With my blushing face.

Cherry A Pietrglciewicz (15)
Lincoln Castle Academy, Lincoln

Video Games

Video games
Full of emotions
Joy, anger and much more
So many communities
So much to do
But so little time to spend
The possibilities are endless!

Brandon Powell (13)
Lincoln Castle Academy, Lincoln

I'm Tired

As young girls we are told to sit up straight
To have to be lady-like at just eight
We are meant to be seen as a trophy
With porcelain skin and cheeks red and rosy
To stay quiet and sweet
And to look skinny and if not... don't eat
A woman is a weapon
For years now we have been threatened
With young boys supporting men like Mr Andrew Tate
I'm tired of all this female hate
I'm tired of the fear of walking alone at night
If we can't see wrong from right, clearly we are not that bright
I'm tired of being told what I can and can't do
I'm tired of waiting for a breakthrough
I'm tired
I'm tired.

Emily Brewer (14)
Radnor House Sevenoaks School, Sundridge

Fighting For Ukraine

What are we doing
to each other?
We're fighting and killing,
It could be your brother!

The kindness is fading,
War and violence sinking in.
No more sharing and trading
Just death and sin.

We try to block it out,
Pretend it's not happening.
Doing stupid things for clout,
Instead of finally accepting the world is shattering.

We're letting people from Ukraine die.
"There's not a lot we can do..."
But would it be different
if it wasn't them, but you?

Jessica Margrett (14)
Radnor House Sevenoaks School, Sundridge

Dreams

Dreams
Hold on to dreams
Because if you give up on dreams
Life seems pointless like a blunt pencil
When someone has a dream they are unstoppable
Like a soldier going into battle
Dreams can be like spaceships
They can propel you above the clouds
They can make you feel as free as a dog in a wide, golden field
Hold on to dreams
If you give up on dreams
Life feels like a frozen lake
One big step and you fall underneath the ice
Gone forever, never to be seen again
Forgotten.

James Paterson (13)
Radnor House Sevenoaks School, Sundridge

War

The destruction of the world,
The depriving of families,
The destroying of land you want.

The destruction of economies,
The death of people,
The sitting back and watching
By the same people who promised you.

Promised you safety,
Promised you help,
Promised you an easier life,
Promised you wealth.

Less taxes,
Less work,
Less stress,
Less hurt.

More time to relax,
More time with family,
More time off,
More happiness.

Oliver Mason (13)
Radnor House Sevenoaks School, Sundridge

Safety

S omeone should help the children on the street
A nyone, anything, that we can eat
F amily, friends, where have they all gone?
E veryone went the minute we left home
T omorrow might be a better day
Y ou should save the children before they waste away.

Alice Watson (13)
Radnor House Sevenoaks School, Sundridge

The Three Men Who Were Never Seen Again

One day, in the deep, dark depths of the ocean there was a small ship
Three people were on that ship: Michael, Franklin and Trevor
They were on a mysterious mission to find out what was really in the omniscient ocean...

These three men all had their own personalities and appearances
Michael had deep blue eyes and was unwise
Franking had a buzz cut and was always in a rut
Trevor had no hair and was always up for a dare

As day turned to night
The whistling wind changed and gave everyone a fright
The three men realised they had been rather naive about their ship's strength
But they decided to stay the night
Eventually, they fell asleep
Little did they know they would wake up to a terrifying treat
As Trevor lifted his head
He realised he was no longer in bed
Franklin and Michael were nowhere to be seen

This is when Trevor heard the screeching screams
The deep, dark depths of the ocean was the least place the three men were ever seen!

Rio Hughes (12)
St Anne's Academy, Middleton

Our Planet

I am here today to talk to you about our planet
The Earth
Do these two words mean anything to you?
The Earth that we were born and raised on
The reason we are here today
Do you really care for it as much as you say and do?
I have walked the streets of our planet
I have watched the people drop their rubbish on the floor
and walk away
Without a care in the world
You, yes you, you are hurting the planet
Bit by bit our planet is becoming weaker because of us
The planet, in fact our planet, has been there for us
Provided for us and this, this is how you repay it!
By murdering it... disgusting!
Soon enough there will be nothing left
No one left
It will all be our fault
We will be responsible for the death of our planet
And for the death of everyone
We will all be murderers.

Faith Sanderson (13)
St Anne's Academy, Middleton

The Happy Place

T hailand has a beautiful culture and future
H ungary has a good Formula 1 track and a lot of packs
E stonia has a good race and ace

H onduras is the 'banana republic' and is very public
A rgentina has the best steak that isn't fake
P araguay has the Pampas fox and bats
P eru has the flu and a lot of shoes
Y emen has a desert and lots of desserts

P oland has the biggest castle and a lot of pastels
L iechtenstein produces good wine and has a lot of pine
A ustria has the biggest ice cave but not a lot of Daves
C anada has the longest street and a lot of concrete
E cuador has a long history of chocolate but isn't late.

Kuba Wasilewski (13)
St Anne's Academy, Middleton

Death Is Inevitable

Death is something beyond imagination,
You don't expect it but it comes after all,
It is horrible but it is the life cycle,
Death is inevitable.

It is something you do not wish for,
But something you end up getting,
You have high expectations but everything shatters,
Death is inevitable.

Death reoccurs from generation to generation and doesn't
stop,
But when it comes knocking there is no way to escape,
No matter your status, it doesn't count you out,
Death is inevitable.

If you're rich and popular, when you die your stories will
be told,
And then they will become history,
And when you die, your world ends and so does your life
story,
Death is inevitable.

Excellent Bright (12)
St Anne's Academy, Middleton

Being Grateful

Being grateful, you have parents
Who support you and your needs
Being grateful, you have a free education
As some children don't even get an education
Being grateful, you have shelter and nutrition
To last you a day, as some people stay
Outside freezing in the cold, staving themselves
Being grateful, you have a home to call your own
Being grateful, you gave freedom in your country
Being grateful, you have money in your bank
Or you even have a credit card
Being grateful, you have a job
Being grateful, you have a loyal friend
Being grateful, you have your health
Being grateful, to take a warm and hot bath, as some
people take cold baths
And sometimes they don't even have a bath.

Serena Ndlovu (12)
St Anne's Academy, Middleton

My Beloved Mother

I am writing you a poem to tell you how much I love you
Something that I always tell
The unquestioning love towards each other is unbelievable
We really do have our ups and downs but truly love each other
You're not just a mum to me but you're my best friend
I don't know how to pay you back for everything you have done for me because you have done a lot
I'm alive because of you
You chose to have me and I'm glad that you did
You have always been there for me like my guardian angel
You care about me and you have suffered your life for me
I love you, Mom!
This is what you are...

M arvellous
O utstanding
M agical.

Anitta Abraham (11)
St Anne's Academy, Middleton

Black Lives Matter

Freedom will not come today or tomorrow
It will only come when we make a difference
People won't stop hating until they realise that this needs
to stop

People won't stop beating up the ones who are different
Not everyone is the same
Some just don't know it
Everyone should be treated the same
People you consider different are just the same as you

People have different skin colours and come from different
countries
But it doesn't mean that they should be bullied
What we need to do is support each other

Black lives matter
Never forget that
Everyone is perfect just the way they are!

Isabelle Barker-Gorse (12)
St Anne's Academy, Middleton

Summer Is Tropical

Diamond air gets hot and thirsty
Basking in the warm summer air
"Taste and drink me!" says the azure salty sea
The air hovers its water and then waves on.

Over land the air is tall and thin
Trying not to heat its toes
On scorching oil this leaves a gap
In which the crystal ocean air now flows calmly and
smoothly.

Bumbling in with bloated clouds
Containing many cups of sea
It slops down exhausted and lazily
Full of damp humidity

But air cannot sit still for very long
As air will move on
So bulging and swollen clouds and summer's noon
Dump buckets of sea in rain's monsoon.

Jacob Nixon (12)
St Anne's Academy, Middleton

We're All The Same

We are all the same
despite all our flaws
We play the same game
even with the same walls

People in this world discriminate
why are humans filled with all this hate?
They care about your ethnicity
but they should practise simplicity
Everyone should have a right
no matter the colour of their skin

I'll stand up and help you fight
those that judge the colour of your skin
Let's work together and we will always win
but the haters won't
You still wonder what they think
even when you're on the brink
Just take some time to say hi
we all live under the same blue sky.

Ilias Papazetis (11)
St Anne's Academy, Middleton

All About St Anne's Academy

St Anne's Academy is the best high school ever
Good teachers, food and lessons
And so, so much more
This school is like a buzzy bee
It is always buzzing
Sometimes the students can be naughty
But I'm one of the greatest (sometimes!)
I'm the person who always finishes first
I always have a smile on my face
I make everyone happy at St Anne's Academy
The lessons are so cool and sweet
Just like the ice cream that comes with everything nice
When you join there are staff, teachers and friends that
help you
They help if you are lost around or in lessons
St Anne's Academy is the best!

Jack Garside
St Anne's Academy, Middleton

How I Love you

Oh, my captivating sage-green
Inspire me to write
How I love the way you memorise
Invading my mind through the day and through the night
Always catching me by surprise
You make me bloom like a daffodil
You are exceptionally pleasing but even more appealing
Fine rain floods the neat fields of April
As your idiosyncratic shade is revealing

How do I love glimpsing you?
Let me count the ways
I love your details, scent and lush
Thinking of your shade fills my days
My love for you sometimes makes me blush

Your shade is just as beautiful as the sky
But sadly now I have to say goodbye.

Oluchi Solomon (12)
St Anne's Academy, Middleton

London

Crime is the fog hanging over London
That infests the innocent Brits
It corrupts the heart, soul and mind
And makes them lose their wits

It is the wrecker of families
And the pain bringer of mothers
It destroys homes
And turns brothers against brothers.

Crime runs foul on the streets
Spreading like a disease
It infects everyone in its way
And destroys everything it sees

But amidst all the chaos and struggling
There shows a glimpse of light
Which inspires those who are willing
And encourages them to fight.

Mcfinley Ngugi (12)
St Anne's Academy, Middleton

The Government's Puppets

The government has slaves
Slaves that we know are us
Like bees at work
All through our lives we get them money
But it's only making the poor stay poor
And the rich get richer
We need to stop being mindless slaves
We need to pave the way for the era of man
The freedom
The system
We are not slaves, we are humans
Humans that should have the power to knock down
the tower of government
Are you with me?
Good, then let us begin...
We are the angels and they are the devils
We are the heart and you are the blood!

Davey-Ryan Parkinson (12)
St Anne's Academy, Middleton

Why Aren't We All Equal?

E xcellent, everyone is excellent
Q uality, everyone has different qualities
A mazing, your goals are amazing to reach
U nlimited dreams, we all have dreams
L earning helps us reach success

R ewind, we can change the past
I ntelligence, you might not think you are smart but you are
G enerous, be more generous
H elping, we can help anyone
T ime, it may take time but we will get it right
S omewhere there are people fighting for rights and we can make it right!

Michael Kershaw (13)
St Anne's Academy, Middleton

School

I'm walking to school with a smile on my face
I meet with my friend
And we go to that special place.
When we get there
I open the door
We walk in our classroom
And there is chewing gum on the floor.
I sit down
Everyone starts to snore
I ask why
And my friend says, "Our teacher is such a bore!"
When it's finished
I look to my right, there are my friends
And they ask if I'm alright.
We have a test, so let's do our best
Even if we snooze
Remember, we will never lose!

Chloe-Louise Heaton (11)
St Anne's Academy, Middleton

Life

In this world, life doesn't stay forever
Life is like a highway
Lost in your own world
Brought out by the pain of the real world
Am I going to survive?
Am I going to survive?
Trying to live through the trap
But there is this feeling that holds you back
Pain running through your veins
You just have to endure it
How am I going to cut through this?
Wondering what to do
If this world ends soon
What is going to happen too?
Life is short, you just have to live it to the fullest!

Damilola Ojolowo (12)
St Anne's Academy, Middleton

Love, What Is It?

"Love, what is it?" I ask you
You think for some minutes before answering
"Love is a set of emotions and behaviours characterised by
passion and commitment!"
"It could be," I reply
I ask an old lady passing nearby
"Love, what is it?"
She says, "Love is the reunion of two souls that are not
complete without each other!"
There are no right or wrong answers
As long as you care for your partner!

Gael Cavezzale (13)
St Anne's Academy, Middleton

The Seven Seas

The waves flow like the air
As the boats flow
As the waves strengthen the fish swim in the wind
But all of a sudden it gets too hot to even swim
But then I see some good food for me to eat
But all of a sudden I choke
I choke until I can't breathe
Until someone so kind sees me struggling
I can't breathe
Again they save me
But as the days go by
More plastic ends up in my home
I hate how I can barely swim freely.

Willow-Kate Crabtree-Deegan (11)
St Anne's Academy, Middleton

A Best Friend

A best friend is like a family
Or a companion
Who is worth more than gold and rare to find

A best friend can change
A frown into a smile
When feeling down

A best friend will understand
Your little trial and lend a hand

A best friend will always share
Their secret and be honest with you

A best friend is worth more than gold
And will give all the life and health you can't hold.

Lola Kalejaiye (11)
St Anne's Academy, Middleton

The Young Boy

The young boy is walking around
It seems like a while
Maybe something's not right
Every day he walks around
All day then something changes
Walking around the stores
He needs something
Tick-tock the time goes
Sometimes he'll return
The young boy is running
It's weird he likes walking
Could something have happened?
Then the young boy is gone
The young boy never appears again.

Jack Nicholls (12)
St Anne's Academy, Middleton

The Importance Of Education

Education is one of the keys to success in the future
Education may be boring but it is crucial
Everybody says that education is an opportunity
To get good grades and you can get a good job
Education is like you are buying something that you can't
buy with money
But you can achieve it and become educated
You can gain a lot of knowledge and help others in need.

Michael Osei Addei (13)
St Anne's Academy, Middleton

I Ride My Horse

I feel the wind
I hear the birds
I ride my horse
As I sing words

I see the grass
I feel the leather
I ride my horse
Upon the heather

I taste the dust
I feel the heat
I ride my horse
To his own beat

I feel great joy
I taste the fun
I ride my horse
Into the golden sun.

Holly Sager (11)
St Anne's Academy, Middleton

The Road Not Taken

A road discovered centuries ago
A person took the road above
The road broke and fell
There was always another path
The path that was not taken
The bricks were collapsing
Tough and impossible to cross
But together we could do it
And the road was crossed
And the road gave a person
A new life
An improved life.

Evangelos Papazetis (13)
St Anne's Academy, Middleton

Nature

The tall old tree was a delight for all to see
The tall green silky grass was showing through the glass
The scent of the rose attacked their nose
They all looked at the azure-blue sky
As they wondered how to say goodbye
The clear shiny water
Reflected the image of my daughter.

Cole Penrose (12)
St Anne's Academy, Middleton

Crazy World

Politicians and people are a war
Over pay, conditions and more
Strikes increase in every way
What more can I say?

No respect or compromise
Where does this truly lay?
Teach the next generation more
And end the divide between the rich and poor.

Joshua Adams (11)
St Anne's Academy, Middleton

Imagine

Imagine a bee
As big as a tree

Imagine a dog
As big as a bog

Imagine a cow
As big as a plough

Imagine a bat
As big as a hat

Imagine me
As bold as can be

Imagine you
As tiny as a shoe.

Pheebe Longshaw (12)
St Anne's Academy, Middleton

My Perfect Day

Stuck at home
Can't wait to get to school
Jump in the pool
Then relax at home
With my homies
Chilling on my bed.

Sima Hamad-Aziz (12)
St Anne's Academy, Middleton

YoungWriters®
Est. 1991

YOUNG WRITERS
INFORMATION

We hope you have enjoyed reading this book – and that you will continue to in the coming years.

If you're the parent or family member of an enthusiastic poet or story writer, do visit our website **www.youngwriters.co.uk/subscribe** and sign up to receive news, competitions, writing challenges and tips, activities and much, much more! There's lots to keep budding writers motivated!

If you would like to order further copies of this book, or any of our other titles, then please give us a call or order via your online account.

Young Writers
Remus House
Coltsfoot Drive
Peterborough
PE2 9BF
(01733) 890066
info@youngwriters.co.uk

Join in the conversation!
Tips, news, giveaways and much more!

 YoungWritersUK    YoungWritersCW    youngwriterscw